ADDRESS

TO THE

SOLDIERS OF OHIO,

BY THE

DEMOCRATIC STATE CENTRAL COMMITTEE.

"THE UNION AND THE CONSTITUTION."

COLUMBUS:
DEMOCRATIC STATE CENTRAL COMMITTEE ROOMS.
1863.

NOTE TO THE DEMOCRACY OF OHIO.

It is of great importance that many thousand copies of this Address should be sent to our soldiers in the army as early as possible. To accomplish this object the immediate co-operation of every Democrat in the State is solicited. All have friends in the army, and by a prompt and combined effort every soldier from Ohio can be reached, within the four weeks that remain.

The following extract from a letter received from General Rosecrans, under date of "Headquarters Department of the Cumberland, Winchester, Tenn., Aug. 15, 1863," in answer to the Committee, is a sufficient assurance that there will be no interference with the transmission of the Address. Gen. R. says:

"As to newspapers, pamphlets and other publications, none have been or will be excluded on the ground of party politics. But I do not belong to that sentimental class who weakly and timidly allow brawling license to stab true liberty. Hence, when any publication appears among us so licentious, lying or traitorous as to endanger the morality or be likely to impair the vigor of the army, I feel bound by reason, justice, and duty to my country, to use my authority to prevent its circulation."

Orders for this pamphlet will be promply filled by the Committee, or by J Walter & Co., of this city.

In behalf of the Committee.

JOHN G. THOMPSON, Chairman.

Columbus, *O.*, Sept. 15, 1863.

DEMOCRATIC UNION TICKET.

LIBERTY AND UNION.

For Governor,
CLEMENT L. VALLANDIGHAM.

For Lieutenant-Governor,
GEORGE E. PUGH.

For Auditor of State,
WILLIAM HUBBARD.

For Treasurer of State,
HORACE S. KNAPP.

For Judge of Supreme Court,
PHILADELPH VAN TRUMP.

For Member of Board of Public Works,
JOHN H. HEATON.

ADDRESS.

Soldiers of Ohio :—We are approaching an election of unusual interest and importance. On the second Tuesday of October next the people of our State must, by their votes, determine the character of our State government for the ensuing two years. Though absent from your homes, as soldiers in the service of your country, you are still, by the laws of your State, citizens. By virtue of an act passed on the 13th of April last, you have the right to add your votes to those of your fellow-citizens at home, and thus aid in forming the character of your State government. That act, entitled "*An act to enable qualified voters of this State, in the military service of this State, or of the United States, to exercise the right of suffrage,*" authorizes those of you who, if at home, would be qualified voters in your respective townships and wards, to exercise the right of suffrage, on the days appointed for holding County, State, Congressional or Presidential elections. While thus absent, in the service of your country, this right is, by the provisions of that act, secured to you as fully and absolutely as if you were on those days present at your usual places of election.

The right thus guaranteed by a law of your State, while an inestimable privilege to you, devolves also upon you a great and solemn responsibility. To exercise the right of franchise wisely, justly, and independently, is, for most men, a delicate and difficult task, under ordinary circumstances. To the soldier in the service of his country, far from home, the difficulty is greatly increased. He is in a great measure deprived of the counsels of his former friends. He is without the advantage of that free and full interchange of sentiment, to which he has been accustomed. He hears none of the public discussions, which to those at home form so important a part of the means of coming to a correct conclusion in regard to the respective merits of the principles and the persons between whom a choice must be made.

But your case is peculiar. You entered the military service to aid in subduing a rebellion, not to find an employment for life, whereby you would separate yourselves from the civil associations and interests of your former homes. Many of you left families, all of you relatives, also circles of friends. And the first wish of those from whom you parted was, that your services might aid in bringing this unhappy and most disastrous war to a just, honorable and speedy termination ; their second wish that you might soon return to enjoy with them the blessings of the peace thus secured. And in order that you might continue to feel as deep an interest as ever in the civil affairs and prospects of your State, they determined to confer upon you through the legislative authority, the right to co-operate with them in the selection of civil officers, both for the State and general governments.

This was a Democratic movement. On the 28th of Feb., 1862, a bill "*to authorize volunteers from the State, in actual service at the time of a general election, to vote wherever they may be,*" was introduced into the House of Representatives by Mr. Dresel, a Democratic member, and a similar bill by Mr. Sayler on the 4th of March, which was referred to a Special Committee—Messrs. Dresel, Converse and Sayler—all leading Democratic members. On the 9th of April ensuing, the Committee reported in favor of the bill. But its passage was not at that time favored by the Republican side of the House. Hence it was laid on the table and not taken up again during that session. But in view of the general popularity of the measure, Mr. Gunckel, Republican, introduced a bill to the same effect into the Senate, which passed that body, but on coming to the House, that also met a similar fate, and therefore failed to pass.

The Democratic State Convention, held in Columbus, July 4th, 1862, condemned the rejection of the bill, in the following strong terms:

"*Resolved,* That the refusal of the General Assembly to permit our gallant soldiers in the field the right to vote, was a great and unjustifiable wrong to them, that ought not to have been committed."

In the fall of 1862 the Democrats carried the election, which was for members of Congress and certain State officers, but not for the General Assembly. In that the Republicans continued to have a majority, but the current of popular sentiment was setting strongly in the direction of Democratic measures. The rejection of the bill giving the soldiers the right to vote was not well received by the people. This the Republican members saw, and at once became the professed friends of the measure, and the bill being still sustained by the Democratic members, passed near the close of the last session by a nearly unanimous vote.

This, soldiers of Ohio, is a brief history of the motives and means which led to the enactment of the law under which you now have the right to aid in selecting the men to fill the executive and legislative offices of our State government. To the Democratic party in whose behalf we now address you, are you mainly indebted for this privilege.

More than half of you when you left your homes were Democrats, and if you were now here with us would undoubtedly vote as we do, and would see the best and most convincing reasons for doing so. You would then know that the Republican papers that have been distributed among you since the war begun, have constantly and persistently misrepresented the motives and purposes of the Democratic party. You would then know that that party is, as it ever has been, the consistent friend of the Constitution and the Union, and has never harbored a thought inimical to either, or to their gallant defenders. The ground on which the party has ever stood and yet stands, is truly declared in the first resolution of its Platform adopted at its State Convention of July 4, 1862, as follows:

"*Resolved*, That we are, as we have ever been, the devoted friends of the Constitution and the Union, and we have no sympathy with the enemies of either."

And why should we have any such sympathy? Every motive that can actuate the human heart leads us to be true to our country, and we have not a single motive to induce us to be false to it. And you will, we feel sure, be slow to believe that that great old Democratic party, that has ever stood by the Union, and to which you have been justly proud to belong, has ceased to be the true party of the country. You will not believe that the fathers, brothers and friends whom you have left at home, have become sympathizers with treason, upon the malignant assertions of their political opponents.

Under these circumstances we have a right to believe you will be true to your own deeply cherished convictions; which must be that the old Democratic party with which you have heretofore acted, cannot be far out of the way. You will surely give much weight to the most reasonable presumption, that if you could be here with us, and be fully informed in regard to all the issues involved in the approaching election, the evidence would be clear and overwhelming to you, as it is to us, that we are sustaining the right measures and the right men.

Our measures have entered into and formed the history of the government, and have constituted the basis on which it has been happily and successfully administered during at least three-fourths the entire period of its existence. That the people of each State and section ought to attend to their own affairs and rigidly abstain from every interference with the rights guaranteed or conceded to other sections by the federal Constitution, has always been a favorite principle with us. The Democracy of Ohio were true to the facts of history when at their State Convention, Aug. 7th, 1861, they declared as the first of their platform resolutions:

"*Resolved*, That the civil war by which our country is at present distracted, is the natural offspring of misguided sectionalism, engendered by fanatical agitators North as well as South; and that the Democratic party having equally opposed the extremists of both sections, and having at all times zealously contended for the administration of the General Government within its constitutional limits, that party is in no way responsible for calamities that have resulted from a departure from its doctrines, and a disregard of its warning and advice."

In the same platform we resolved:

"That the volunteer soldiers who, at the call of their country, promptly went forth to do battle in defense of its Constitution and Laws, and who, in many cases, have been compelled to fight under inexperienced officers, are entitled to our hearty thanks for the gallant manner in which they have discharged their duties."

Again, in the PLATFORM adopted at our State Convention, July 4th, 1862, we declared that

"The history of the Democracy is a record of unceasing and unvaried devotion to the union of the States; ever fulfilling the injunction of the Father of our country, to 'cherish a cordial, habitual and immovable attachment to it; accustoming themselves to think and speak of it as of the palladium of their political safety and prosperity, watching for its preservation with jealous anxiety; discountenancing whatever might suggest even a suspicion that it could, in any event, be abandoned; and indignantly frowning upon the first dawning of every attempt to alienate any portion of our country from the rest, or to enfeeble the sacred ties which link together the various parts.' "

At that time we also resolved,

"That the Abolition party, by their denunciation of the President, when ever he has manifested a conservative spirit; by their atrocious defamation of our Generals who were exposing their lives for their country, and who needed and merited its hearty support; by their acts and declarations tending to promote insubordination in our armies, and a want of confidence in their commanders; and by their persistent representations of all conservative men in the loyal States, as sympathizers with the rebels, have given immense aid and comfort to the rebellion, and encouraged them to hope for ultimate success."

We recorded our most solemn and unqualified condemnation of the emancipation policy, and in doing so, gave the following among many other reasons:

"Because such an emancipation would throw upon the border free States, and especially upon Ohio, an immense number of negroes to compete with and underwork the white laborers of the State, and to constitute in various ways, an almost, or quite, unbearable nuisance, if suffered to remain among us. And we would deem it most unjust to our gallant soldiers to see them compelled to free the negroes of the South, and thereby fill Ohio with a degraded population, to compete with these same soldiers upon their return to the peaceful avocations of life."

In the same Convention, we said:

"That while we will, as heretofore, discourage all mere factious opposition to the Administration, and will continue to give our earnest support to all proper measures to put down the rebellion, and will make all the allowances that the necessities of the case require of good citizens, we protest against all violations of the Constitution."

And at our State Convention, on the 11th of June last, we declare in our *platform:*

"That the soldiers composing our armies merit the warmest thanks of the nation. Their country called and nobly did they respond. Living, they shall know a nation's gratitude; wounded, a nation's care; and dying, they shall live in our memories, and monuments shall be raised to teach posterity to honor the patriots and heroes who offered their lives at their country's altar. Their widows and orphans shall be adopted by the nation, to be watched over and cared for as objects truly worthy a nation's guardianship."

The platforms and resolutions in which the above and many similar sentiments are expressed, have been printed in all the Democratic papers of Ohio. Hence you know what position we have occupied in relation to the war, and to all other questions in which the welfare of our country is concerned. We quote the above passages to bring to your memory, and place immediately before you, a few of the leading principles and purposes of the true and genuine Democracy of Ohio, the firm and unwavering friends of the Constitution and the Union.

OUR CANDIDATE FOR GOVERNOR.

To lay fully before you the claims of the Hon. C. L. VALLANDIGHAM to your suffrages and ours, and to give you a full explanation of the reasons that have determined us and the great mass of the people of your State to elevate him to the office of Governor, would require more space than this brief Address will permit us to use, in that way. We regret that this is so, as you are thus deprived of your just right to be fully informed in regard to every fact and every principle involved in the important issue now pending.

Against the other candidates on the Democratic State ticket, no serious objections have been urged by the Republican party. Their fitness for the offices to which they have been nominated, on all save political grounds, is generally conceded. But against Mr. Vallandigham you have heard many grave charges, among which are, that he is a "*disunionist*," "*an enemy of the soldiers*," "*a convicted traitor.*" If any of these or of the many other equally damaging charges were true, that fact would constitute the best of reasons why you should not give him your votes, while we, for placing him in nomination for the office of Governor of our State, would be justly disgraced in the estimation of all honorable men.

Our answer to those charges is a bold, positive, unequivocal denial of their truth. Mr. VALLANDIGHAM is not a disunionist, an enemy of the soldiers, nor a convicted traitor. On the contrary, he is now and has been at all times, through the whole period of his political career, in every speech, and every act of his life, a firm, able, and consistent friend and defender of the Union. To repeat every speech, and mention every act by which he has labored to secure the constitutional integrity and permanency of the Union, and protect it from the disastrous consequences of sectional strife, would require a large volume. There is no statesman in this country, nor has there ever been any, whose labors in that direction have been more constant and unremitting.

Sentiments tending to encourage disunion were introduced and advocated in the Ohio House of Representatives, by certain abolition leaders, as early as 1847. Mr. VALLANDIGHAM, then a member of the House, was among the first to rebuke and denounce those sentiments. In a speech on the 22d of January of that year, he said:

> "That whenever any question might arise, involving the Union in the alternative, *he would go with his might on that side*—ON THE SIDE OF THE UNION, 'NOW AND FOREVER, ONE AND INSEPARABLE.' Would any gentleman relinquish the Union rather than tolerate the existence of slavery in the South?"

Again, on the 2d of September, 1847, Mr. V., on assuming the editorial charge of the Dayton *Empire*, said:

> "We will protect and defend, according to our opportunities and abili-

ties, THE UNION OF THESE STATES, as in very deed the 'Palladium of our political prosperity,' 'the only rock of our safety,' less sacred only than Liberty herself; *and we will pander to the sectional prejudices, or the fanaticism, or wounded pride, or disappointed ambition, of no man or set of men, whereby that Union shall be put in jeopardy.*

And on the 27th of June, 1849, when relinquishing the charge of that paper, he again said:

"That *which is really and most valuable in our American liberties, depends upon the preservation and vigor of* THE UNION OF THESE STATES; and therefore, all and every agitation in one section, necessarily generating counter agitation in the other, ought, *from what quarter soever it may come*, by every patriot and well-wisher of his country, to be 'indignantly frowned upon,' and *arrested ere it be 'too late.'* "

On the 26th of October, 1850, at a large Democratic meeting in Dayton, Mr. V. reported a series of resolutions concluding thus:

"That 'all obstructions to the execution of the laws, all combinations and associations, under whatever plausible character, with the real design to direct, control, counteract, or awe the regular deliberation and action of the constituted authorities, are destructive of the fundamental principle of our institutions and of fatal tendency; that all such efforts, wherever made or by whomsoever advised, find no answering sympathy in our breast—nothing but loathing and contempt—and that we hereby pledge ourselves to the country, that, so far as in us lies, the UNION, THE CONSTITUTION AND THE LAWS, must and shall be maintained.' "

In a speech delivered in the House of Representatives, Dec. 15, 1859, Mr. VALLANDIGHAM said:

"Is it not, I appeal to you, better then for you of the North, better for you of the South, better for us of the West, better for all of us, that this Union shall endure forever? Sir, I am for the Union as it is, and the Constitution as it is. I am against disunion now, and forever."

In the same speech he also said:

"Mr. Clerk, I am, not, perhaps, so hopeful of the final result as some other men; but I was taught in my boyhood that noblest of all Roman maxims—never to despair of the Republic. I was taught, too, by pious lips, a yet higher and holier doctrine still—a firm belief in a superintending Providence, which governs in the affairs of men. I do believe that God, in his infinite goodness, has foreordained for this land a higher, mightier, nobler destiny than for any other country since the world began; *Time's noblest empire is the last.* From the Arctic ocean to the Isthmus of Darien; from the Atlantic to the Alleghanies; stretching far and wide over the vast basin of the Mississippi, scaling the Rocky Mountains, and lost at last in the blue waters of the Pacific, I behold, in holy and patriotic vision, ONE UNION, ONE CONSTITUTION, ONE DESTINY. (Applause.) But this grand and magnificent destiny cannot be fulfilled by us, except as a united people."

On the 20th of February, 1861, Mr. VALLANDIGHAM said, in the House of Representatives:

"Born, sir, upon the soil of the United States—attached to my country from earliest boyhood, loving and revering her with some part, at least, of the spirit of Greek and Roman patriotism—between these two alternatives, with all my mind, with all my heart, with all my strength of body and of soul, living or dying, at home or in exile, I am for the Union which made it what it is; and, therefore, I am also for such terms of peace and adjustment as will maintain that Union now and forever."

This declaration occurs in that famous speech in which Mr. V. is said to have proposed to divide the Union into "*four distinct nationalities.*" Such is the assertion repeatedly and persistently made by the Abolition press. There could not be a more direct perversion of the plain and obvious meaning of language. It must be a bad cause that requires the aid of such means. Every one who has read the speech and the resolutions that accompany it, knows that the proposed division into "*four sections,*" upon which so much stress has been laid by the Abolition papers and speakers, refers simply to a proposed change in the manner of taking the vote in the Senate; this and nothing more. It did not in the slightest degree contemplate dissolving the Union. Its purpose was to preserve it.

No one has more firmly and consistently opposed every movement or sentiment looking to disunion. And he has firmly opposed every movement aiming at peace on the basis of separation. His resolutions, introduced into the House of Representatives on the 16th of December, 1862, exhibit correctly his views and the character of his efforts in relation to this matter. The first three are—

"*Resolved*, 1. That the Union as it was must be restored and maintained forever, under the Constitution as it is—the fifth article, providing for amendments, included.

"2. That no final treaty of peace, ending the present civil war, can be permitted to be made by the Executive, or any other person in the civil or military service of the United States, on any other basis than the integrity and entirety of the Federal Union, and of the States composing the same as at the beginning of hostilities, and upon that basis peace ought immediately to be made.

3. "That the Government can never permit armed or hostile intervention by any foreign power, in regard to the present civil war."

The remaining three are in harmony with the above.

In a speech at Hamilton, O., September, 1862, accepting the nomination for Congress, Mr. Vallandigham said:

"At your demand, therefore, men of the Third District, I accept the nomination, and present myself to the people for their suffrages, upon no other platform than the Constitution as it is and the Union as it was."

And such sentiments have characterized every speech, vote and act of his political life.

At the first appearance of that deadly struggle which is still wearying the life and consuming the substance of the nation, Mr. Vallandigham was among the most earnest and active in every honorable effort either to avert the coming storm or so to guide it that it might not leave the wreck of the Union in its track. In nothing he has said or done, in Congress or out of Congress has he ever counseled or attempted the interposition of any unconstitutional or unlawful hindrance to the prosecution of measures adopted by the Administration, but has uniformly counseled a full and implicit obedience to all laws when enacted. No man in the Union has stood more firmly against every sentiment that would encourage an uprising of the people in defiance of laws, even when unpopular and obnoxious.

On the 12th of July, 1861, he said in Congress:

"For my own part, sir, while I would not in the beginning have given a dollar or a man to commence this war, I am willing—now that we are in the midst of it without any act of ours—to vote just as many men and just as much money as may be necessary to defend and protect the Federal Government. It would be both treason and madness now to disarm the Government, in the presence of an enemy of two hundred thousand men in the field against it."

In his speech in Dayton, Aug. 2, 1862, he said, speaking on the subject of enlistments:

"Whoever among the Abolitionists would curse secession, let him enlist, and then he will show his faith by his works, and your armies will be full in a week. Let every man who would invite others to go, first go himself. I have never interfered with enlistments. While the war lasts, our armies, for many reasons, must not be disbanded; so I said in Congress more than a year ago. Without enlistments they can not be kept up; and if any man, subject to military duty, really thinks that the Union can be restored by force and arms, and only in that way, let him enlist; it is his duty to enlist; he is 'disloyal' if he does not enlist. Whoever shall be drafted, should a draft be ordered according to Constitution and law, is in duty bound, no matter what he thinks of the war, to either go, or find a substitute, or pay the fine which the law imposes; he has no right to resist, and none to run away."

On the subject of supplies for the army, he said in his speech in Congress on the 14th of January last:

"The country was at war, and I belonged to that school of politics which teaches that when we are at war, the Government—I do not mean the Executive alone, but the Government *is entitled to demand and have, without resistance, such number of men, such an amount of money, and supplies generally, as may be necessary for the war, until an appeal can be made to the people.*"

And again, in the same speech:

"I could not, with my convictions, vote men and money for this war, and I would not, as a Representative, vote against them. *I wanted the President should take, without opposition, all the men and money he should demand, and then to hold him to a strict accountability for the results.* Not believing the soldiers responsible for the war, or its purposes, or consequences, I have never withheld my vote when their separate interests were concerned."

Mr. VALLANDIGHAM has uniformly done all in his power to secure for the soldiers in the service of the Government, just and liberal payment and bounties. In a letter to his constituents, under date of May 13th, 1861, he said:

"Waiving the question of the doubtful legality of the first proclamation of April 15th, calling out the militia for "three months," under the act of 1795, I will yet vote to pay them, because *they* had no motive, but supposed duty and patriotism to move them; and, moreover, they will have rendered almost the entire service required of them before Congress shall meet."

And he did thus vote. When on the 9th of July, 1861, the bill appropriating the sum of six millions for the payment of the three months volunteers was under consideration, Mr. VALLANDIGHAM not only supported it, but in reply to a remark of Mr. Stevens asking the House to give its unanimous consent to the passage of the bill, Mr. V. replied: "I presume there is no objection to the bill at all."

In answer to a letter, dated Hamilton, O., Oct. 6, 1862, Mr. VALLANIDGHAM said:

"In reply to yours of yesterday, I have to say that I supported all the measures in the last Congress looking to the giving of invalid pensions to all soldiers 'wounded or incurring disability in the military service.' Upon a question like that, no just or humane man could hesitate for a moment. Every soldier who has performed service is entitled to the pay and bounty promised him by law, and all disabled in any way during service are entitled to pensions; and I have never, either directly by vote or indirectly by refusing to vote, withheld either, where the service had been rendered or the disability incurred; nor would I do so."

On the 2d of December, 1862, an effort was made in Congress to increase the pay of soldiers to fifteen dollars a month. Mr. VALLANDIGHAM took an active part in the movement, and proposed to "*make the fifteen dollars payable in gold.*"

The above statements indicate clearly and correctly the position Mr. V. has occupied in relation to the support of the army. He has been at all times the firm friend and defender of the rights and interests of the soldiers, when drafted or enlisted into the service. He has always maintained that they were justly and fully entitled to every compensation promised by the government, and has on several occasions endeavored to secure an increase of that compensation. Many of the soldiers know and appreciate the value of his services in their behalf; and if they could all be permitted to know the full and true history of what he has done and endeavored to do for them, there is no one for whom they would cherish a stronger affection. As a general fact, the interested misrepresentations of enemies, war contractors and abolition disunionists, are the only reports in regard to Mr. VALLANDIGHAM that have obtained a free circulation in the army. This cannot continue much longer. A deep and stern sense of natural justice guides the popular will, both in and out of the army, and sooner or later forms the controlling sentiment.

Not only has Mr. Vallandigham been charged with giving his whole sympathies, and, as far as possible, his influence in aid of the rebellion, but he has even been accused of devising and favoring invasions of the Northern States. Great efforts have been made to fasten upon him, both among soldiers and civilians, the odium and prejudice of this most damaging charge. As these reports, together with their pretended proofs, must have come to your notice, we will allude to a few of the more serious.

On the 31st of July last there appeared in one of the daily papers of this State a leading editorial under the heading "*Vallandigham in* 1847 *and* 1861."

The article commenced with giving some account of Mr. V.'s course in regard to the war with Mexico, alleging that he had given that war his cordial sympathy and support, because it was waged in the interest of slavery, quoting also a resolution, in relation to the prosecution of the war, offered by him at a Democratic meeting held in Dayton, Dec. 18th, 1847. The article then says:

"The man whose voice was then all for war, is now attuned to peace on any terms. The man whose soul was then fired against poor, helpless Mexico, now gives all his cordial sympathies to the South. The same man who in 1847 uttered the words of the foregoing resolution, in 1861 uttered these words:

" 'Then, sir, I am not a Southern man either, although in this most unholy and unconstitutional crusade against the South, in the midst of the *invasion*, arson, insurrection and murder to which she has been subject and with which she is still threatened—with the torch of the incendiary and the dagger of the assassin suspended over her, *my most cordial sympathies are wholly with her.*' "

Of the above quotation, the article says:

"Mr. Vallandigham uttered this in 1861, and nobody doubted his sincerity. His whole course of conduct, public and private, authenticates the sincerity of his statement that his most cordial sympathies are with her (the South)."

Portions of the above words, said to have been uttered by Mr. V. in 1861, are again turned over, repeated and commented upon, and the reader reminded that the *incendiaries* and the *assassin* are the *Union men.*

The item thus started has had a large run in the abolition papers. In several instances the quotation from Mr. Vallandigham has been accompanied with remarks reaffirming and repeating the assertion that the speech in which the passage occurs was made in 1861, and refers to the present war. One remark, which has been moving around in connection with the passage and as a commentary on it, says:

"Thus as early as 1861 did this detested traitor, Vallandigham, array himself against the Union cause, and commence anathematizing the brave soldier boys. * * * If he thinks he will secure a support in the army, he is much mistaken. Soldiers will not vote for a man who brands them with such epithets as *assassins, murderers* and *incendiaries.*"

Now the truth is that the passage is taken from a speech delivered in Congress on the 15th of December, 1859, MORE THAN A YEAR BEFORE THE WAR COMMENCED. The allusion is to John Brown's raid into Virginia, the general subject before the House being the fitness of Hon. John Sherman for the Speakership, he having indorsed and recommended the Helper book, which was supposed to be a part of the secret history and hidden machinery of the said John Brown's raid. And yet strange to say those unscrupulous enemies and defamers of Mr. VALLANDIGHAM, have manufactured that base slander and spread it everywhere, asserting that the speech was made in 1861, and in reference to the present war.

On the 14th of February, 1863, Mr. VALLANDIGHAM delivered an address in Newark, N. J., in which some of the New York papers falsely charged him with saying,

"It has been proclaimed that it never was the Confederates' intention to invade the Northern States, yet if this war is kept up, battles fought, no relenting spirit, no prospect of peace, no sound of concord to reach our ears, *they ought to be induced to make that invasion.*"

Mr. V. immediately addressed a note to the *Tribune*, under date of New York, February 16th, correcting the erroneous report, saying,

"What I said as to invasion from the South was, that 'if the war was kept up with no relenting spirit, and no prospect of peace, *they might possibly attempt invasion of the North and West*, and then we would write for them precisely the history they have been writing for us during the last two years.' "

This agrees with the passage as given in a full report of the speech published in the *Freemen's Journal* of February 28th. And yet that false report has been kept moving, although, in addition to the correction in the newspapers, Mr. V. explicitly and positively denounced it as false from his place in Congress, and repeated what he did say.

This absurd report belongs to the same class with that stupid and malignant falsehood in which Mr. V. was charged with having said, at an Ohio caucus in Washington, December, 1860, that "before Federal troops should be permitted to pass through the Miami Valley, they must march over his dead body;" a charge which has been thoroughly exploded and exposed on Republican authority.

In a speech, accepting the nomination for Congress, September 4th, 1862, Mr. VALLANDIGHAM offered the following, which was adopted by the meeting unanimously, amid great cheering:

"*Resolved.* That it is the highest duty of the citizen, whenever his country or State is invaded, to rush to its rescue, by arms, if he is capable of military service, and by money or otherwise every way, if he is not; and that the Democracy, as a part of the people of this district, laying aside all party feeling for that purpose, are ready with life and fortune to do their part in discharging this patriotic duty."

Such have been Mr. V.'s sentiments at all times in relation to any possible or proposed invasion of the Northern States by the rebel armies. No shadow of a thought written or uttered by him in Congress or out of Congress ever has been or can be produced which, even by implication, looks like inviting or favoring an invasion of the Northern States. A charge of this sort would be too absurd for denial, were it not that it has been and still is repeatedly and persistently made with a bold and reckless tenacity of falsehood. Either the men who make this assertion believe that a lie well stuck to finally becomes a truth, or else, which is more likely, they hope to make a large number of people believe those base and damaging charges.

We have thus, Soldiers of Ohio, placed before you a few facts and statements showing the high, honorable and statesmanlike course pursued from the beginning and at all times by the man whom the Democracy of your State have placed in nomination for Governor, and whom the people, with an almost unanimous sentiment, with an enthusiasm unequaled, have determined to elect to that office. No election ever held in this country has been regarded with deeper interest; none has involved more momentous issues. Never have the hearts of the people, of all ages and classes, been more deeply moved.

In the election or defeat of Mr. VALLANDIGHAM a great principle is at stake, aside from the question of his fitness for that important office. The course the administration has pursued in his case and the position it still occupies are in direct conflict with the theory and practice of this government, as understood and applied by the Democratic party.

Our views on this question were thus expressed, in our State Convention on the 11th of June last, when we said:

"*Resolved*, That the arrest, imprisonment, pretended trial, and actual banishment of Clement L. Vallandigham, a citizen of the State of Ohio, not belonging to the land or naval forces of the United States, nor to the militia in actual service, by alleged military authority, for no other pretended crime than that of uttering words of legitimate criticism upon the conduct of the Administration in power, and of appealing to the ballot-box for a change of policy—(said arrest and military trial taking place where the courts of law are open and unobstructed, and for no act done within the sphere of active military operations in carrying on the war)—we regard as a palpable violation of the following provisions of the Constitution of the United States:

"'1. Congress shall make no law * * * abridging the freedom of speech or of the press, or the right of the people peaceably to assemble, and to petition the Government for a redress of grievances.

"'2. The right of the people to be secure in their persons, houses, papers and effects, against unreasonable searches and seizures, shall not be violated; and no warrants shall issue, but upon probable cause, supported by oath or affirmation, and particularly describing the place to be searched and the persons or things to be seized.

"'3. No person shall be held to answer for a capital or otherwise infamous crime, unless on presentment or indictment of a grand jury, except in cases arising in the land or naval forces, or in the militia, when in actual service in time of war or public danger.

"'4. In all criminal prosecutions, the accused shall enjoy the right to a speedy and public trial, by an impartial jury of the State and district wherein the crime shall have been committed, which district shall have been previously ascertained by law.'

"And we furthermore denounce said arrest, trial and banishment, as a direct insult offered to the sovereignty of the people of Ohio, by whose organic law it is declared, that 'no person shall be transported out of the State for any offense committed within the same.'"

That arrest was also a most unjust, cruel and unmerited impeachment of the loyalty and patriotism of the Democracy of Ohio, and a poor return for our unmeasured contributions of treasure, service and life. On this subject we also said, at our State Convention :

"*Resolved,* That Clement L. Vallandigham was, at the time of his arrest, a prominent candidate for nomination by the Democratic party of Ohio to the office of Governor of the State ; that the Democratic party was fully competent to decide whether he was a fit man for that nomination ; and that the attempt to deprive them of that right by his arrest and banishment was an unmerited imputation upon their intelligence and loyalty, as well as a violation of the Constitution."

Accordingly, in pursuance and defense of our just rights, which you, as soldiers of Ohio, will not desire or expect us to relinquish, we resolved :

"That we respectfully but most earnestly call upon the President of the United States to restore C. L. Vallandigham to his home in Ohio ; and that a committee of one from each Congressional district of the State, to be selected by the presiding officer of this Convention, is hereby appointed to present this application to the President."

The committee thus provided for, and consisting of nineteen chosen men of Ohio, repaired immediately to Washington City, and in a personal interview, also by a written memorial, respectfully but most earnestly asked the President to revoke the sentence of banishment and permit our candidate to return to his home. In closing a clear and able presentation of the case the Committee said, in behalf of the people of Ohio :

"In their name, we ask that, by a revocation of the order of his banishment, Mr. Vallandigham may be restored to the enjoyment of those rights of which they believe he has been unconstitutionally deprived."

In reply the President did not attempt to justify or defend the banishment of Mr. VALLANDIGHAM on the ground that he had been convicted of treason or had committed any crime known to the laws. He said the arrest was for "*prevention and not for punishment.*"

The sentence was not revoked ; Mr. VALLANDIGHAM is still an involuntary exile. But the Democracy of Ohio have resolved to assert and maintain their constitutional rights and the dignity of their State by electing him to the office for which he has been nominated. And you, Soldiers of Ohio, are interested, equally with us, in maintaining the rights guaranteed by our Federal and State Constitutions. Those rights belong to every citizen, and when violated in the person of any one citizen, all are assailed. If Mr. VALLANDIGHAM may be banished in defiance of the Constitution and the Laws, then may any other citizen be banished in like manner. And if this can be done, who is safe? You desire when you return to civil life to be secure in person and in property. Then stand by the Constitution and the Laws which guarantee that security. Vote the Democratic ticket, and when you return to your homes you will have the satisfaction of remembering that in this contest you took the right side.

Your friends and fellow-citizens,

JOHN G. THOMPSON, *Chairman*,
A. G. THURMAN,
AMOS LAYMAN,
S. MEDARY,
GEO. L. CONVERSE, *Secretary*,
Democratic State Central Com. of Ohio.

COLUMBUS, O., Sept. 15, 1863.

www.ingramcontent.com/pod-product-compliance
Lightning Source LLC
LaVergne TN
LVHW020638110826
845149LV00004B/1271

* 9 7 8 1 4 1 8 1 9 0 2 4 8 *